heft

Also by Doyali Islam

Yūsuf and the Lotus Flower

heft

DOYALI ISLAM

McClelland & Stewart

Library and Archives Canada Cataloguing in Publication

Islam, Doyali Farah, 1984-, author
heft / Doyali Islam.

Poems.
Issued in print and electronic formats.
ISBN 978-0-7710-0559-6 (softcover). —ISBN 978-0-7710-0560-2 (EPUB)

I. Title.

PS8617.S53H44 2019 C811'.6 C2018-903249-9
C2018-903250-2

Published simultaneously in the United States of America by McClelland & Stewart, a division of Penguin Random House Canada Limited.

Typeset in Arno by M&S, Toronto
Printed and bound in Canada

McClelland & Stewart,
a division of Penguin Random House Canada Limited,
a Penguin Random House Company
www.penguinrandomhouse.ca

1 2 3 4 5 23 22 21 20 19

Penguin Random House
McCLELLAND & STEWART

for you whose body has slipped through a crack

– contents –

poem for your pocket

astro-poems

split sonnets

double sonnets

parallel poems

ok

postscript

poem for your pocket

poem for your pocket

what my pockets have kept over seasons:

coffee change. house keys. ttc tokens.

emptiness and silence and my ungloved

reticent hands. poems. thoughts of miklós

radnóti—he who hid in his pocket

a thin notebook on his forced march toward

death in some unallied forest.
forced

beyond reason to one mass grave, one mass
silence. still, one silence his overcoat

pocket would not keep: eighteen months
passed before his wife unpacked that pocket

of earth—rifled through corpses, clothing—found
what remained. it was love. love rifled through

miklós's silences—love gave his damp
last pages back to sunlight's keep. oh yes

yes, it was love announcing in him, *i*
will find my way to you, i will come back.

hid [redacted] den [redacted] is a chronic [redacted] occlusive [redacted] characterized by recurrent, painful, deep-seated hid[redacted]den [redacted] is frequently misdiagnosed as [redacted] this results in delayed diagnosis, fragmented care, and a progression to

astro-poems

ok

jane & methuen, outside golden gecko coffee

two nights before you (gemini rising)
decide we're long-term incompatible
because our astrological charts don't align
& henceforth become known, between daniel
& me, as *astro guy*, we're on our first
date, walking bloor west village for hours.
hours in, your four-year-old daughter calls—calls
again, wanting to be sure you heard her say,

i love you.

no hesitation—you offer it back,
cradle softly your smartphone, softer still
this phrase which, offered once by my father,
might have rendered useless so many years
of therapy.   you are
bare & sweet with each other, bare
& sweet like the maple-lined streets twined with
light, being, as it is, three weeks before
christmas. & christmas being the season
to believe (in something, anything),
i choose belief in the power of the word
vicarious—this moment managing
to fill a gap that probably led
to okc in the first place. & because
when has my dating life ever turned out,
i decide, for once, to be prudent &
selfish—to take this one thing, store it away
for winter, here in this poem, this ledger
of tender; because, well, trust a libra
(with jupiter in capricorn) to keep account; & because
i need to be left with something.

aries [the ram]

here is the threshold i do not cross—natasha trethewey

there once was a king. he married
the cloud goddess nephele who bore him children:
a daughter, helle, and phrixus, a son.

when the king took a second wife [jealous
of his progeny], he sharpened a knife
and raised it high on mount laphystium

over the boy's neck, as helle looked on.
it would have been done but with pleading
zeus answered the prayers of the mother

[or was it the mother answered her own
prayers] sending down a wingèd golden ram
for their escape.
though

if you, father, were not born stubborn ram
and i, libra: an opposition, distance
circumscribed by a zodiac. i tell

the story again: there once was a ram,
but in this, our earthbound version,
only a kitchen is golden [yellow fluorescence];

the ram, unharmed and warm in his own fleece
pajamas, save the fact that he's choking
you're choking

on a tablet, clutching a cup at the sink,
and i am nearby, within helping distance—

my right hand made fist
for some manoeuvre
or
do i hold the balance

helle
fell,

phrixus survived and sacrificed the ram
back to zeus—its bright coat nailed to an oak
in the grove of ares; nephele raising its fleeceless

body to the stars.
all this to explain how a ram came to be
on some nocturnal tablet, related to an obdurate

patron of quarrels.
so says ovid or apollonius
of rhodes or maybe wikipedia.

i admit none of this would matter

the judgement on your life?

this is the threshold i do not cross—my arms
afraid to embrace, to dislodge
something long stuck in your throat.

so here we are, ram and daughter, frozen
each to our place—a tableau vivant of reticence
as you choke.   father, forgive me my fault.

somewhere
high above this kitchen ceiling
justice rushes a starry vault; her scales,

dropped.   a clatter—

sagittarius {the archer}

you are tortured by the serpent's blood—ovid

the gods were punishing prometheus
for something—theft, or generosity.
he was bound to a rock in tartarus,
jupiter agreeing to free him if
a suitable replacement could be found.

let's be real:
it wasn't looking promising;
and each day, in the meantime,
some huge eagle
kept claiming the titan's liver,
after each night of it growing back.

{since we're on the subject,
can we talk about that?
i have a theory:
maybe, maybe,
the eagle had issues
—anaemia or some kind of autoimmunity—

how this relates to sagittarius
has to do with a centaur, chiron,
renowned for his compassion and all-round
excellence. . . .woe to this immortal horse-man!
his name, in greek, meant *skilled with the hands,*
yet even he couldn't heal himself
from one particular wound;
so, in his chironness, offered to make use
of his irresolvable pain by switching places with prometheus.
jupiter was moved by this,
and gifted him a bit of sky.   sister,
being sag, you might want some more deets,
like who wounded chiron, and why. it was
an accident:
heracles had been trying to stop
some other centaurs from drinking his wine.
he was shooting at them with venom-dipped
arrows—the venom from a hydra that had proved
hard to kill. . . each cut-off head sprouting

and, well, there was p,
with his presumably good-quality, previously free-range
liver. . . .what if, for centuries,
we've focussed on crime and punishment,
civil disobedience, and necessary defiance,
when all the greeks wanted
was for us to eat more organ meat?}
but

two new heads {which is how
writing poems sometimes feels}.
. . .in the night sky, the tail of constellation hydra
lies between centaurus and my sign, libra—
but what if that's backwards,
the serpent's head near me? i am sorry
by proximity, and for accidents
of my blood.

virgo (the virgin)

terras astraea reliquit—ovid

1

my mother isn't sure when she was born.

human error—her father recording
22/02 and *22/09*
in the date field on separate documents.

two cheesecake opportunities! two zodiacal choices
but, for my part, i think of my mother as virgo
rather than pisces.

first, there's the fact that virgo is linked to
astraea, daughter of
eos (titan-goddess of dawn), and that
my mother's mother (a poet)
took for her pen name *nurun nahar,*
which emits, from the arabic, daylight.

2

sometimes it upsets me, libra that i am,

that my celestial rep rises no higher than
inanimate object,
pitiful scales among sea-goats and archers and bulls.

worse, that these scales only manage to remain up there,
floating in that narrow band of night,
because of the neighbouring hand of

astraea.   (if not you, o anxious mother,
couldn't ptolemy have granted me
a bit of independence? but then
what did the man know anyway
claiming all celestial bodies
revolve around the earth.)   and maybe

second, that astraea, who found herself
on earth, was the last immortal to leave it,
last to abandon humans and their small cruelties
for the interstellar.

my mother did not wish to abandon
her mother—that daylight—
for my father and the stars
of this darker, colder
country,

but she did.

and when her mother was dying
—all that water between them—
my mother wept beside me in the night,
unable to afford a plane ticket home.
i was six. i abandoned her
to her grief.

it's the damn scales that make me
so sensitive to the burdens of the day—each day's
tiny cruelties bearing down on my skin,
which is a skin of witness.

maybe it's because i'm libra and my mother virgo
that sometimes when night falls and i ride the bus home
walcott's woman visits me
—not the young beauty, the light of the world,
but the older one with the heavier
basket.

i am that basket.

? is it past or premonition
when i hear the bearer plead, *pas quittez moi*
pas quittez moi

à terre.

scale

burnhamthorpe road

my mother and i walk home from market
with leeks and lettuces, apples and a basket
of peaches. she is concentrating
on her half of the load,
refusing to let me take it, and so
does not see what's up ahead: a sparrow,
or, what once was a sparrow, when it flew.
i know: scale is a cardinal sign,
usher of autumn, hinge that swings open
the door of death, but the bird was struck,
lies mangled on a driveway,
and i fear it—angle my hinge-body
between sorrow and sight.
if grief can be weighed, my mother has borne
more of it, and what if torn wings tip
the balance, render life unbearable?
my hands are human, mostly unable
to restore anything.

a chronic, disabling [redacted] a profoundly negative [redacted]

[redacted] exact etiology of hid[redacted]den[redacted] is unknown. [redacted]

split sonnets

jelera

upon the sloping green, the men stand, bared,
the old and young sharing ordinary
sunlight, their waists draped with cotton lungis.
there! by the water's far edge, an old man,
alone in his swim and drag, crossing through.
his white crown solemn and dry above the murk,
he is the keeper of the net—and hands

it over only when he's swum his length.
then each man moves, makes distinct his longings,
plunging into the weight and worth of carp—
most thrown back like salt over the shoulder,
swift disappearance into the deep pool.
hear the flurried utterance, see the white churn,
and each slippery body—a memory.

contract

between plastering & priming the ceiling,
you tell me about something that happened
in struga, where you grew up. somebody
had a heart attack & was taken
to hospital. doctors called the partner,
who was out buying bread, & her heart, too,
constricted. both died within the hour.

you named your business for your son, albion,
but *yellow pages* claimed it was common,
so you dropped the *o*. is everyone trying
to close the gap between themselves & what
they love? my hairdresser, llisa,
untangles again & again the knot
of one question—llarge, her llove of llamas.

trip to yarl's wood

2006

her village is like a mouth unpainted.
she plots its edges, she plots its edges.
a woman lining a lip with colour,
she spares the henna of her body.
her thoughts and feet lead to women: new brides
whose backs arch like new moons, and the old ones
who still season the fūl madammas pot.

the shadow long in front of her is her
vision, and she pursues it—or rather
it pulls her body along the dirt road:
an animal plodding, tied to its load.
a man will stick his knife in her belly—
see the scar like the fringe torn from a skirt?
! what a seed of sorrow and non-return.

visit to a thrift shop

2006

i can't remember which london corner
but i remember the brown corduroy
making something of my legs as she searched.
not purses, but knits. . . .outside, winter streets
hold shuffling figures close for passing warmth.
in a mirror a face not quite hers sees
her, searching too. *when will you return?* she
turns, once again leaving, left. knows she is
already forgetting the charge of her
mother's eyes, their colour like karkade
steeped in evenings. what this language would call
hibiscus. she sleeps between fits and wakes
to the tv on the wall's other side.
she knows it muffles grief, and points to it.

water for canaries

july 26, 2014

the a.p. photo shows two men of beit
hanoun. during the ceasefire, they had gone
back to what they called home to find their birds
alive amid debris. one pours with fraught
hands from a bottle: it's a small-throated
mercy, surviving a strike from the air.
but which photo can recall the deft

quiet fusing of clavicles into
one auspicious fork—bones hollowing—the
sprout of feathers—? no memory of the long
flight into their bodies—the last singing
descendants of a burning world—the first
heirs of a new, they preen in their pink cage.
their bodies emanate fine clouds of dust.

confronting global change

university of toronto

last requirement i need to graduate
so instead of komunyakaa and keats
i'm learning hadley cells, trophic states, plate
tectonics, and the k-pg boundary.
from her lectern, professor tutty's voice
drones: *an asteroid left dinosaurs extinct.*
i scroll through world news: cement in gaza
now fifty dollars a bag—the going
rate on the black market. one man, 'imād,
has found a way to rebuild his home with sand,
gypsum, and limestone. between the clicks of
powerpoint slides, i dream seafloor shells, bones
stirring in walls: forgotten, lithified
things buzzing, buzzing beneath a drone's wings.

moose hunting

north bay

it is an easy thing to hunt a moose
when it stands stock-still in a field—the kind
boys play ball in, before a shrill bell
calls them. it is an easy thing to cover
arms, legs, in black; take just the keys; hurry
down leonard, champlain, to schoolhouse grass
where late-night dog walkers have just brushed past

a moose, their cigarettes tarring his rack.
like love—easy to hunt, but not to find:
a bell waiting to be struck, struck, is how
we waited—but the moment long over-
turned, so we turned back. for what had we come
except the furred bell at his throat? its great
silence ringing out against smaller ones.

cat and door

for poncho

one night, as i came in, the brightened hall
opened to him /   / he saw, almost dared
to stride, sensed his limits, and his eyes were wide.
i shut the door. so there he crouches,
a creature in my mind, bent after new thought.
was it inevitable, the key thrust,
the turn? i remember his pleasure at

a bird's call / her *ti-litt ti-litt* / how all
of him leapt like light to light returning.
darkness soon curtained, curtailed, his vision.
was it a dutiful hand or a cruel
master who gave glimpse of that golden wing?
did he live by it, or die by it?
solidness suddenly a hushed measure—

moving day

north bay

tomorrow my hand will shake as the key
turns in the lock and all the rooms empty
of our sight. we'll have packed the air mattress,
emptied the fridge; the day good for a drive.
springtime—and heading south in the u-haul
the land ahead will rear, rise. you will call
it a *horst* and explain how we'd lived

at the edge of one—this ridge, the other.
the wheels will rumble across the graben,
that low stretch where the land was humbled by
glaciers. primed by a terrain of *normal*
fault and *rift*, the word *divorce* will still split me.
halted in traffic, i will ask you why
eros clings to *erosion*, *birds* to *debris*.

shirt

seen at the nuyorican, from the row behind

a high-backed blouse.
navy; stitched with sequins, crystal, and pearl.
a garment that seems a firmament or
a season of its own.
decked,
i decide; the toggle switch of recall
suddenly flicked,

thrown:
a frost-wrought silence; my wrists
laced with an absence
of heat as i carry bread through a december night; each porch
fixtured with green and red, blue and white. which is to say,
i am outside. which is to say, *a hunger*
or *a texture like longing.*

vulva

sometimes i think of myself as *pippin*
and my vulva as *merry*. i hold him
when he asks, *are you going to leave me?*
like in the third *lotr* movie
when he's half-dead on the battlefield
on the outskirts of minas tirith
whose castle promontory, let's face it,
looks like a giant clitoral hood hewn

from stone. pippin finds his merry—
to his question, replying, *i'm going*
to look after you, which means, *no, merry;*
you are not expendable.   i don't know
if battle i've been through—what i or my mother survived; what passed to me
as muscled terror and an anger at my body.
that my clitoris is forged like a wish-
bone, like yours, is a sign of some survival.

v

if i publish this poem, absurdly
i imagine no one will overhear
that what i have is called *vaginismus,*
that i have learned pleasure within constraint
or just beyond it—a supra-vaginal
superwoman. still, it is super hard
to find a man content with the non-
penetrative life. i guess i gave up
years ago on dilation; couldn't pass
the third or fourth size; never found the worth
of intercourse, that brand of openness.
i thought this fact made me super abnormal.
i thought i'd given up on my v, but
it was just the world's idea of it.

homecoming

after w.s. merwin

i'm listening to a youtube interview
of the poet w.s. merwin.
two davids are with him as he recites
"homecoming"—the one about the plovers,
half their weight gone to get them home, heaving
their yearning. and as the notes rise from his
throat like dark, curving, plangent wings against

the moon of his forehead, hair white as the
ermine whose fur belongs to winter's own
coat, i know i will rewind this over
and over—by which i mean *re-wind it.*
for a moment, the kitchen has stopped
its cleavings, the tv from afar its *war*
and *oil, hunger* and *fire.* hunger, and fire.

in johnstone strait

afternoon. how long you eyed the surface
those hours in the johnstone strait. you held still.
everything churned under the tent of sky.
everything in your world turned liquid
and returned to its womb; the colossal
mountains reduced by mist to their outlines;
those, sharpened. of course, it happened as your
face turned away: dorsal fins sundering
steely waters; then heads and flukes; then whole
black-and-white bodies arriving in air,
lacquered like some better language. something
glacial, moved by its own weight, split your heart.
curtains of water fell. do you recall,
for an instant, the narrow things widening?

letter

to anyone who is listening

lately my despair is so great i can
barely stand up beneath it—for the moon
& the drone hang in the same sky, while tolls
a voice, *from my mother's sleep i fell—*.
some days all i wish is to be reborn
into a stronger body—one larger
& more buoyant; durable as

the giant kelp. kelp me would be fibrous,
would have a holdfast; & when you'd say,
tell me of black smoke, tell me of rubble,
i, in my kelp body, would simply sway.
at home in cold waters, the turbulence
of your questions would bring me nutrients
for my survival. it would sustain me.

sleet

burnhamthorpe road

at weddings, my uncles used to say,
you look like your mother. i was sixteen,
wearing her old saris and my hair down.
of the saris, my favourite was simple:
blue and purple georgette, raindrop pattern.
it was my father who bought it for her,
and i will give him this: the man had taste.

did precipitation and a colour
claim her? she carried milk through february snow
as dark uncoupled from dark at her temples.
her palms were callous-laced; her coat purple
like the first stubborn signs of spring. damp nights
like tonight, are my hands and knees my own?
a driver lowers a ramp; i carry groceries home.

bhater mondo

for my mother

my mother used to make little rice balls
for me. she steamed and clattered about the
cramped mustard kitchen, filling a pot with
water, swelling and salting and songing
the grains, plating them like planets longing
for some lost centre, chirping, *my mother,*
o, she made me small small bhater mondo.

one morning away from ringing school bells
in fourteen perfect globular mouthfuls
she fed me her story, and uncooked dreams.
and although my fingers cannot craft rice
they do cling stickily to the grain
of history, ever remembering le monde—
the world of sacrifice between her hands.

anise tea

at jericho

raouf's hands as he measures the anise
are seeded with fragrant losses.
from somewhere in the back, in his corner
of the glebe, he fuses lime and honey:
a collision of geographies—three
exiles in one cup. when these histories
have steeped enough, his right hand bears the weight.

always give with the right hand—the right hand
blesses, my mother used to say, her mouth
sterner than the hand that served us lentils.
raouf's from yāfā—balata—palestine:
his past remade, framed, on these bank-street walls.
if tea spills, it spills. small catastrophe.
it can be absorbed. he can remake it.

tending mint

january 4, 2009

in a baseball tee and tracksuit bottoms
kamal awajah tells one behind a lens
what happened after the soldiers
left him in his street, his boy's torso shot
like his own. they must have been slow—so slow
the hours his son's breath waged final trespass.
he cries, and i hear his story as snow

settles on northern-ontario silence
six years on. his roof's still rubble.
near a tent, he tends mint in ibrahim's
honour, and the bullet nests—a halted
flaw within his chest. nothing, it seems,
can demolish his gentleness. even now,
light salvages itself in his eyes.

hymenoptera

i wanted to write about bees in this
book—how they enter into a sohbet
with rose: the ears, pearls, buzzing in her throat,
emerging with nectars of unsaying.
but i couldn't. the ants kept arriving.
look down: small black figures, motions on ground,
born to the earth and not distinct from it.

i wanted to write about bees in this
book—how they make and share a rare sherbet,
a dense clarity hiding in our world.
but darker ones swarmed into light, out from
the underbrush, in common work. those who
find life in the dirt and rot of discard,
i give myself to these tough-footed ones.

[redacted] rupture [redacted] ruptures [redacted] rupture [redacted] rupture

rupture

double sonnets

susiya

for the nawajah clan, and others

in the south hebron hills the slanted hills
recall old songs, and the women collect
them like rain. the men have two-syllable
names—'azzam, yūsuf, khaled, nasser—each
name (from their fathers and their grandfathers
before) a dark foot binding them to the
land. they tend sheep and honour the resistance
a windpipe gives a blade. when the machine
arrives with its yellow claw, the clan sings
thalāthīn nijmah—a love song
for the hills. khaled's throat is a dry well.
if he could split his tongue in two, he would
stake half in the earth and tend a singing
tree, a slim upward band of green with fresh
water from places they knew. now they camp,
and memory is an urgent neighbour.
but just as hope seems severed from hope, one
amongst them lifts the *shabbābah*—the old
six-holed flute severed from pvc pipe.
feet spring up on fevered earth: ten pairs of
hands are clapping, and sara nawajah
at seventy is dancing, the slim green
band at her waist turning circles with her.
see the embroidered white cloth streaming from
behind her head a flag in the absence
of olive branches? see their jaunty
shadows, long in afternoon's light, knocking
upon a fence, asking it for a dance.

the ant

i pointed to the creature on the floor:
the one hauling a burden, a rice grain;
the one who had come from a sunlit wood.
such a slight thing, to fear its composure.
my father's eyes followed my gesture through
to its visible end, and his hand placed
a cup over the fraught form. so, it traced
the perimeter of its plastic cage,
wondering at the hard unseeable edge,
hurrying to make sense of its enclosure.
his hand tore off a piece of envelope
and slid the white scrap under the cup.
then the ant was a black mark on a page,
struggling to interpret its situation,
while we spoke over it, opening a door.
so too, one day, will he be ushered out,
back into brightness in which once he stood,
a slight thing exiting a hooded world,
a smallness held close by someone like me,
the white scrap laid over, in quietude.
but before he passes that ringless gate,
tunnelling through a belt of mystery

—which is to speak of the journey of ants—

he'll have looked for a burden all his life—
something to heft, heft for nourishment;
something to pain him and free him, at once.

light

april 7, 2017

standing on a plastic stool, my father
changes the bulb in the ceiling fixture
in the den. having aged, he no longer
bothers to dress; lives in sets of pjs
that sheathe him in diamond-like patterns. still,
the rigour of a former engineer:
each twist staccato and measured until
edison screw cap comes loose from socket.
my vantage point is from below: from here,
scarlet shells flutter down through dim
air—last repose discarded with the lamp.
they died in their quest for warmth, but others
camp—set up homes in the room's wide corners.
the man is no saint but with moth,
spider, ant, or beetle he is tender
as an underarm revealed through repair;
his *den,* a true *denn* (old english for *lair*).
maybe for him it is easier to love
what is not his by blood, what seeks only
passage or refuge.

tonight, he works quietly while the tv
conjectures: *what is to come* (more hunger,
danger) *for the syrian people?* his
pjs, amid the garish sound bites, seem
patterned not with diamond but with missile
crosshairs,

tracking and targeting a land
not his own. ladybird and tomahawk
have both rained down, and bbc *waits for dust*
to settle—speaks in the interim of
crisis, risk. my father listens but reaches
beyond full height—one hand closed around
a new bulb. i see him as counterpoise:
left arm (slack); right arm (raised); right hand (a fist):
silhouetted in doubled dark, he is
intent on his chore—until the light,
the light is restored.

site

on tuesdays in the cramped mustard kitchen
i tear open a swab, pull the white cap
from a vial, screw tight a syringe's halves.
his sight is back—clouded lenses plucked out—
so i'm cautious as i spy the thin jut
of elbows; white shirt under which sutured
skin hides what the tumour took—a backbone
now of stainless steel, an internal cast
of rod and screws. look: he keeps an empty
chai packet stashed in his breast pocket
for the good scents of cardamom and clove.
my mouth is stern: i pretend not to love
the needle's bevelled tip, its hollow
gluttonous guzzling. neupogen funnels
like sand through a timer's slim neck. my hands
each week grow steadier than weather.
they drain the little bottle faster,
develop a square and useless pride.

the nurse mapped his skin, pointed to the sites:
abdomen (at least two inches away
from the navel); the back of the upper
arm (right or left); the thigh (never chosen).

the nurse told me to hold it like my pen.
she warned, *be swift*.
he kept calm, gave us nothing.

but she was not there when, at the picnic,
someone said between bites of pie,
you've had a good life, and the shade of those
five words passed over his eyes. on tuesdays
he who would never laugh or cry or tell
a joke or work all the days of my life
learns to mouth *thanks,* and *please*. that's when
i'm the closest i'll ever be to him—
both hate and love the place i enter in.

flare

1	2
brief.	*flare. flare-up.* as in, *chronic, recurrent,*
	to which doctors and google say, *no cure.*
	flare (classed *mild*) which yields no hospital stay.
	flare during which i wish someone would stay
what issues from a firearm, a pistol.	close—a good pair of arms, a chubby cat.
	flare which, aside from xylocaine, one grins
	and bears, letting what swells and suppurates
	swell and suppurate.
blaze of light, signalling distress at sea.	hidden flare for which no one brings flowers;
	onset upon which i draw curtains,
	shut out the day.
	10/10, flare inflamed by terror.
solar. what nasa classifies from *b* to *x*.	10/10, flare which rhymes with *despair.*
	flare which i defy to fling back curtains,
	drink water, go walking in woods.
	flare that unflares, momentarily, among
a short pass (football). a weak fly (baseball).	wildflowers and friends:
	mary on the trail in front of me
	quick to declare her love of purple vetch;

late-'90s mark of popularity,
which my jeans did not have.   light,
unsteady, glaring.

tyler, behind me, quick to quip, *mary,*
stop trying to make vetch happen; it's not
going to happen. (this welcome kind of flare
perhaps closest to the 17th-century
to shine out with a sudden
light.)   *flare,* as in, *sudden outburst of anger*
toward one's own body; wretched body
that i look at, when i dare.   this body
that means, *i'm alive, i'm surviving,* but which
i am trying to survive.

moving

1993

squished into the back of a minivan,
my mother, my sister, and i. us three;
passenger left empty—a depression
in this landscape, vanscape; a placeholder
for *father, depressed father, my father.*
twenty-six years, and still i remember
our driver—an *ed*, an accuracy
verified by my mother, whose diary
supplies this square filipino realtor
a surname: *shosha*. at seven,
i'm not sure how to spell it, but it sounds
hushed or rustling—how the late-spring night feels
between showings, and how we move through them:
each 30 seconds, devoid of lingering.

in the minivan, ed asks my mother
what she does for a living—a question
so casual and usual he does not see
our bodies stiffen; the grand houses
we're viewing in tension with our actual
situation. *accounting*, she offers,
hiding the truth of telemarketing.
all these years
all these years
i've not once heard my mother
ask for succour, and this backseat-night we
humour her—weigh each place's merits; ours
for the choosing. through darkness—buckled, hurtling—
just for a moment, we are moving.

two burials

millwood park

i once saw a she-goat give birth to twins.
well, in truth, i fled the delivery
but saw the blood and placenta marking
the worn stall when i swept the chèvrerie
of its filth. yes, it was spring when i saw
one kid with ears of brown velvet die slow
in a straw-filled crate in front of a wood
stove. i had gone to the french pyrénées
to learn what life was like—and when her small
body no longer stirred, the farm-kids' wails
went up like smoke. an operatic pall.
i was reminded, then, of another
day—closer to home but just as foreign—
when 2 girls dragged solemn feet through autumn
led by a man with a brown paper bag.
days before, it had held some grilled delight
but now betrayed something cold: a weight
that might have been a clementine—the kind
mothers pack their children for school. i think
now of him among shadows and oak,
he whose hands carried to the woods that sack
and bore the stiff, unassailable
load until the earth claimed it back. not once
had he fed the creature, refilled the glass
tube with water, or changed the pungent felts
of her bed. yet he stood in a clearing,
with sunday best and grave words, to mark
a tiny passage and a grief, still furred.

she testifies

2015

she grew up beside me

our bodies grew contoured together
mingling firm and fluid, water and earth

his feet followed hers. he
                    followed the old seam and spl/
                    it her like cotton. spl/
          it h/
     er over and ov/
     er. i could do nothing
                    but run. his stone
     girth
     sunk
     deep

                              as a broad/
               axe. his veins taut as telegraph wire

     some pieces
               he left in the bushes

for other wolves. the rest, with me
expected my silence to conceal her
but like glass, i drove her fragments to shore

and didn't that boy bobo wash up just
the same, sixty years since?—well not just
the same: tallahatchie bleeding red while
big mil and roy try burning his crepe-
soled shoes. a huge backyard bonfire! three hours
they're at their festivities. they try, try
everything, but the damn thing just can't lie
dead/ he's bobbing up, his black neck tied with barbed
wire, his bloat speaking with more force than
carolyn bryant. …some boys are fishing, gossamer
lines skimming water. his gun-shot skull, a bowl
offering water. later, an open casket.
mamie wringing out his name. it's emmett.

sites

mill road

1

spring cleaning—and in the great purge i find
a postcard marked *jeddah a.p.* and stamped
11 - 8 - 1987

almost 30 years have passed since you left
for what should have been a six-day affair
to the holy sites, calling, *i am here,*

o lord, i am here: two lengths of white cloth
as your only cover, and your peppered
hair unshorn. now, i imagine you there,

as she must have done in those months before
your return (with beard long and a slim reed
toothbrush in accordance with muhammad's

2

today we set out to salvage what light
we can by tramping a path through late
afternoon: you, in brown socks and sandals,

your good trousers, and cotton t-shirt.
our shadows punctuate this road like breath
punctuates our bodies. because i see

your shadow fatten, tumour-like, i say, *look,*
silverthorn's tree. (one autumn we gathered
the fallen, fly-bitten pears to knock down

better fruit.) we walk, and i want to share
what i wish you had known—that love is built
not found and, like faith, cannot announce, *i*

ways): circling en masse a dark, glittering cube
or passing seven times between two hills.
you must have been on your knees, then, in search

of pebbles to throw at three stone devils
which reminds me now, *like cures like*—is that not
what homeopaths say? our world made

plausible.
doctrines of signatures, light.

am here, without a measure of doubt…
bread becoming what it is only through
hunger. dare i say it as we enter

your favourite dollarama and you wheel
the cart 'round for biscuits and bread? yes,

one tree and a cheap store: these are the sites
to which we roam—which our feet together
sanctify before pointing us home.

amble

markland wood

1

annual community garage sale,

and my father and i hunt for deals

in markland wood: a set of salt & pepper

shakers, a pair of trousers, a stainless

steel pot. late may, the streets already

humid and fragrant;

green trees offering shade and occasional

wonder—japanese lilac with showy,

creamy panicles. we pause; we amble;

2

home: good-value shakers on the table;
their bottoms stuck with small oval labels
that read,
elegance® silver plated on brass
an elegance which, o hypomanic father, you attest
in our cramped kitchen, your confidence backed
by dexamethasone.   this is how
someone's junk becomes our "elegant shakers,"
christened by script and your tongue—
the whole afternoon-evening praising,
          elegant, elegant
                    a clipped-off,
brassy, two-dollar mantra while you
grind black flakes to dust, elbow-jut as the pestle
works.   *elegant, elegant*
                    no doubt,
a mind attuned to beauty, a listening with eyes,

all the while, my thoughts on glass and cloth,

steel, and the edgy-earthy

scent of pepper.   of what

are you built? what bits of language formed you?

what was it you ingested,

from mother or sister or friend?

all i can think of is my father, his voice

a blunt blade discarding most things with,
meaningless,

or calling dollarama bread *good value.*

only a bit less keen than our listening long ago
(your game of winding the analog clock
—the kind discarded at sales like today's—
one minute unspeaking,
each of us recording what we heard…)
father, it took me 20 years to discover
what was pointed to: not the sounds of a world,
but the silence beyond them,
the way our shadows on sidewalks point back
to light, more than to the objects in between.
i wonder if you knew—knew too well—
about light and silence, as i'm trying
to reconcile how a mind like yours
chose engineering over verse.   perhaps
to listening you were
too attuned, as to a durable otherworldly
call—and so could find
no makeshift refuge
in language, could not value my brief plunge.

geesturing

or, stopping by woods after work; north bay

of the cream and copper underside; of
the minute needling space with its sleek brash
head as the wings beat a path through air; of
the slender neck, a dark finger pointing
to itself: something quickens, a silence
stirring us both. for a fraction—really
just a momentary stilling, the space
between two ticks, the blood swelled between flaps—
its shadow and mine motion together,
a shape gathering itself, doubly darkened
but not doubly burdened. how the brain shrinks
beneath this flocking sunset, shrinking like
a black walnut going back to seed. would
i ever be so sure, something called home?

the woods are always closer than we think.
the sky is blue. the sumac in the bush
is red. it swerves yet is steadily there,
that black line by now so far above me.
like the edge of a voice alternating
—now soft, now harsh—my ear tracks it still. it
holds itself up to the last judgement of
light. this contrast in me swells to friction—
like a body awoken from slumber,
freshly caught between dreams and the shivering
dark of a room while something small ticks. would
such a body go back to sleep, to its
old season? each year, it stays later, feeding
on something. i do not ask to see.

nightfall

or, the other half is silence

nightfall
being turns cochlear. an ear
a rose

a crowd diminishes

hazard a call. listen
as your heart echoes back
its longings

tomorrow
a luminous turning
will be your body
abandoning all fear

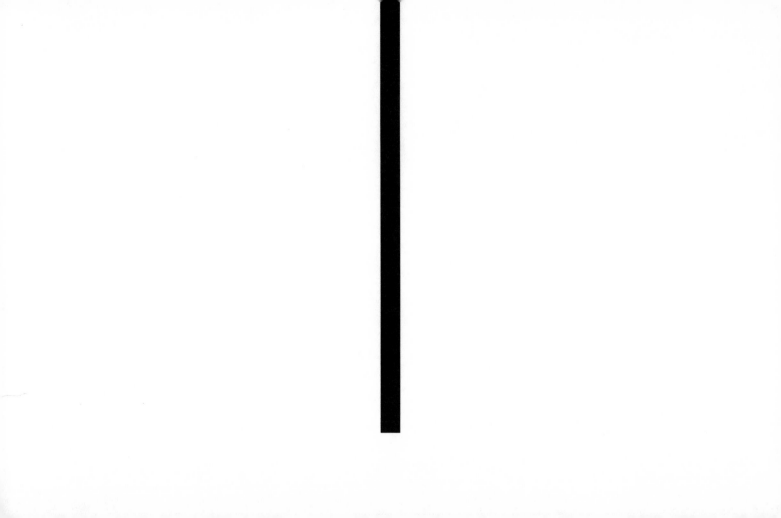

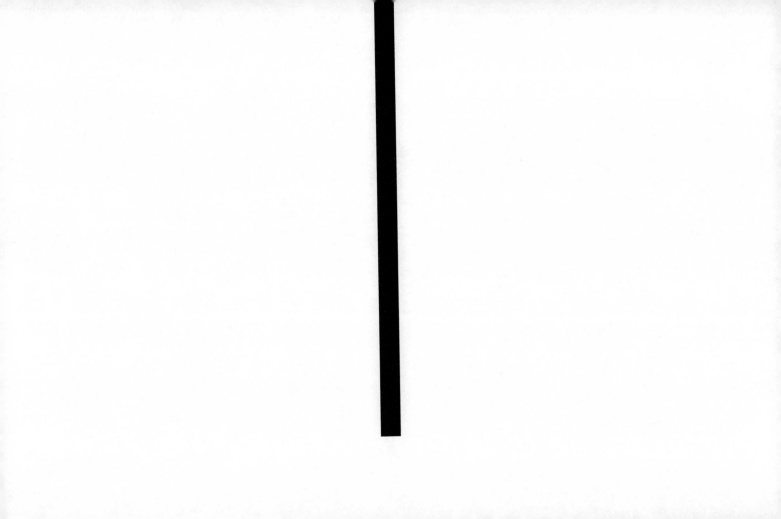

parallel poems

– 43rd parallel –

2016—sunnybrook, toronto 1

this city, a paradox
of plasma and gloves

to know a name, to never see a face

she waits and counts how fast cells settle
she notes what is bioconcave, what is sickled

amid hum and clap and unspun din
squash and push, microscopic
vision: her head bends to her work

what is more intimate than this communion? breath hovering over
blood and spicules, fluids peritoneal and synovial
(collected aspirations of a city)

she finishes her shift, leaves behind
a white lab coat's certainty and the unknowable
pleural griefs, erythrocytic angers

2 capezio, toronto—1988

she is a poet, so
of course she sells shoes

by which i mean she spends her time

trailing and convincing wealthy customers
not to buy, and dusting while thinking of rimbaud

on break, she reapplies
her mac lipstick (a sultry red wine)
drafts an ad on scrap receipt paper

wanted:
young & economically virile
patron of the poetic arts

she pays *now magazine* 45 dollars
for a print in the classifieds
(no one responds to her call)

the 11, the 34, the 20 to kennedy
busloads
of skin hunger

jostle, a seat, the weight of a stranger's
head nestled on her shoulder: an accident

of fatigue and proximity

to see a face, to never know a name
a paradox, this city

drinks at bemelmans
consolation
past midnight

deep-green satin blouse, black mini, smoky eye:
subwayloads

of truncated desire

she sells shoes and is a poet, too
familiar with desire

– 42nd parallel –

buhl 1	2 depew
when you found me, you called me *grindelia* or *gumweed,* but, like ms. lucille's poet crab, you cannot feed me my secret name.	she don't have to do nothing she don't want to.
call me *vulnerary*: i heal wounds. call me *poultice* if you find me clothbound.	
give me the worst dirt; give me dry waste: i will suckle that earth, make myself at home.	she don't have to do nothing she don't want to.
lens shaped & closely toothed, what can i say? i am hungry & made for looking.	
so what if i am sometimes ornery? everyone is allowed this.	she don't have to do nothing she don't want to.
my leaves & buds are sticky, sticky. who doesn't want to be resinous?	

come close.

approach, & find your hands
covered with gum:
i have no respect for soap & water.

she don't have to do nothing she don't want to.

– 41st parallel –

burlap and canvas

santiago to chicago 1

they took my son from here.

i said

i'm his mother; you have to tell me
what's going on.

they told me

not to follow or i would pay
the consequences,
but i kept going.

2 mataro to leghorn

vulgar latin: *cannapaceus*—of hemp.
more recently, of linen or cotton.
used for traditional wedding marquees,
a heavy-duty fabric, plain woven.
thread wefted over and under the warp.
oil paintings; material stretched

across frames—tension upon which art builds.
cordage (more specific than *rope*).
lateen sail, windsail. sails raking
passage.

? is it true bolger said of the lateen,
most graceful (from *a la trina*—of triangles;
latine in an 1841 message
from leghorn: *on the 3rd of january last,*
a sharp, fast-sailing vessel, or bovo,

arrived in this port from mataro,
this *on the coast of spain. she is rigged with*
latine sail, latine sail, and spreads;
in all about 2250 yards of canvas.
is where the truck was; they threw him *she clears out for havana*
into the truck. i was going *with water-casks for ballast; and, it is said,*
to climb in the back. *irons, rings, boards for divisions, &c.)* most
as i grabbed the truck, graceful. before boat building, he had studied
one of them hit me. another one kicked me, history, but the draftsman must have forgot. i can't

and can't forget marta ugarte
and i fell. who washed herself up on another shore,
wiry and more durable than what
concealed her. *o aparecida*
that's when i began to unravel you had been a dressmaker.
unravel my sweaters, your hands, small in life,
stitch questions were very large and had
into burlap. no fingernails.

– 40th parallel –

boulder caravan 1	2 harlem sestina
my passion	i don't know why
for nature (and i went to school for visual art)	you haunted my thoughts, refused to be silent
sort of all merged together	after headlines faded—even now sighing, *i am islan nettles*
into natural building and making creative homes that aren't,	*i am she : i am he* *whose breasts still*
aren't just houses, but actual art pieces	*bear the stress of a crime they won't name*
that people can live in	*as hate (i don't care what they do, i just don't wanna be fooled,*
through living in a space, you're actually sculpted	is what the man said in his plea to avoid full
by the environment:	trial) why
the sculpted environment actually influences	the man (named
the way we present ourselves in the world; it's like	james) did what he did had to do with rage or fear so salient
a second skin.	he broke nose, jaw, eye socket, skull—and still
you wanna grow into	everywhere is islan nettles:
your second skin	islan nettles
and put intention into it, so that you're becoming	(risen for her own vigil) among little candles in foil
your house, in a certain way	tart pans; islan nettles outside 1pp (her face a black-and-white still);
	nettles prickling the mouth of a mother who asks, *why?*
there's a bit of a disguise in the outside	and, *how do you sleep at night?* of the assailant
the inside is where i put my energy	who assailed after asking, *where you from, girl? what's your name?*

they're all reclaimed things: a lot of this stuff you wouldn't notice,
but with a special eye and accenting its beauty,
really appreciating the tree branch for what it is,
i feel like i've shown its beauty in that way

and not only
is it the natural materials, but i've,
i've really intentionally made this
a womb space,
creating this
circular feel

i made a contraption:
the bed hugs you in.
you can really feel like you're being cradled… that comforting
environment of being held while you sleep

when i come home, it's to be nourished,
and part of that safety is having a soft
environment to rest into… there's been studies
that corners and edges put on a part of our brain that shows there's danger.
so by curving the environment, not having
corners, it creates a safe environment for you
to, to rest in

your satin voice at west 148th and 8th proclaimed, *my name*
is islan nettles—
the mermaid whose dark hair streams black
the merman in his unarmoured body who fails
always to armour

after the headlines faded, i searched online to drag up the name
i s l a n n e t t l e s
compelled, without knowing why,

to reclaim those letters as *taintless, lintel, lisle, listen*. why,
698 words rise like allies or birds from i s l a n n e t t l e s
to salvage, to salvage your name

– 39th parallel –

on preservation

lesbos 1	2 pyongyang?
as ink fades, please hide this fragment	what matters beyond the extraordinary
no memory of the long	way bandi's manuscript was smuggled out
flight into their bodies	was that for twenty-four years it was kept
in your body	in a cupboard

– 38th parallel –

each half to be read aloud by a different person, alternating lines

state of missouri vs. darren wilson, grand jury, volume v 1	2 act v, *macbeth*, lady macbeth in the voice of darren wilson
from everything we have always been taught	out, damned spot! out, i say!—one: two: why, then,
about blood,	’tis time to do’t.—hell is murky!—fie, my lord, fie!
you don’t want it on you,	a soldier, and afeard?
you don’t touch it,	what need we fear who knows it,
you don’t come into contact with it.	when none can call our power to account?
thinking that i was cut	yet who would have thought the old man to have had so much blood in him.
with someone else’s blood on me,	the thane of fife had a wife: where is she now?
i had to wash my hands.	what, will these hands ne’er be clean?
so i go directly to the bathroom.	no more o’ that, my lord, no more o’ that:
i actually washed them, went to the bathroom	you mar all with this starting.
and then i looked, like i still had it in my cuticles and stuff,	here’s the smell of the blood still:
so i washed my hands again.	all the perfumes of arabia will not sweeten this little hand.

– 37th parallel –

samos 2 1 kuşadası

when we were on the sea, after 5 minutes i remembered
we don't have life jackets. suddenly the engine stopped.
the captain tried many times to restart the engine,
but it didn't start again. everybody was shouting;
everybody was crying. little children, women, men. i
was thinking about my mother. after a few minutes, the
water was very rough. there was a hole. the water was
coming from the bottom. the boat turned over, and we
were sinking. i was holding my mother. in the water,
i get unconscious. i'm
really angry at myself. why
couldn't i rescue my mother?

– 36th parallel –

mondavi 1

after leaving mondavi for paris

camus wrote of sisyphus:

that hour like a breathing-space

which returns as surely as his suffering,

that is the hour of consciousness

2 burial at kobanî

if you must choose a burden, choose

one that nourishes, drives you home:

ants know this, and all who

in longing

haul the burden of love

– 35th parallel –

in tehran 1

she nibbles zereshk shrouded in ziploc
her blood   the red of barberry juices for
home   quickens, privately and inwardly

desiccated   pvc-capsuled   erythrocytes
crisp   ethnic vacuum (like quarantine)
displaced amongst polow-grain bodies

in tehran sanctuary must keep silence
under domed tiles of trucked turquoise
seal her off from zikr for unbroken blue
sky and a merciful sun that lets tears be

a collapsed mountain: her body   slumped
unreservedly ranges nowhere, crosses
angled streets   an 18-year-old parched
in the fabric of self dyed invisible   she
in khorasan reverie covers dry sorrow
saloms with two university mates in farsi

2 to kyoto

she rises dead   rice-bran bar soaps nose

cheeks, forehead, and chin   pressed with

pond's double white   dolled, porcelain

black sugilite and cultured pearl gaze

glazed   stockinged legs in flared ebony

skirt;   pumps tick time   curb sleepiness

to j.r. wakayama train station   between

seaport and arashiyama mount scope her

dream   for two hours to kyoto university

kurmanji quashed at elementary degree

this tongue   learning the self-silences
with a *hesh-hesh* sound   shifting rubble

her arms crane inwardly from shoulders
to scoop up her heart   crumbled identity

without mountains, there will be no kurds

(gap chromatic)   contrasts   made-up   self

she dwells between bottom half and face

: pulses naked   resisting all clothing

umi no mono tomo, yama no mono tomo tsukanai

– 34th parallel –

2018, going with grace, los angeles 1

a death doula
helps a person who is dying
plan for their death and

supports the family through it.
it's the most invigorating,
life-affirming thing i know how to do.

talking about sex
won't make you pregnant;
talking about death
won't make you dead.

i'm not comfortable
with other human suffering
if there's something i can do about it.
we suffer alone a lot,

2 pigee's beauty shop, clarksdale, 1961

at the close of day, it's not dime
i count though i'm proud to own it
but the number of well-worn places
where women can stretch to easing,
learning to sit inside their power

white or non-, the men don't enter
neglect that power is best divided
that this makes it stronger—like
fistfuls of hair to courage plaited
or the pass-around of chitlins 'n maw

that quickens our throats to a song
and fills us with longing for more

as with any she-activity, men call
this work *so tedious*, but when you

and i don't think we have to.

my funeral?
what i'd really like is to be outside
in my orange raw-silk shroud.
one day

you and i will die,
but before that day comes,
let us live. let us live, let us live.

gather yourself up, head set fine,
reading the resistance in your own
cheek, your bone and blood, i grin

sometimes the mirror catches us in
and not liking what you see, i say,
it's just one version of the truth
inexact in its mirroring 'n afraid
to look 'round itself—and anyway
you have to account for distancing

– 33rd parallel –

1947 - 2008, ehime 1

wooden sandal : three lines solid
| |

: between the teeth breath

wooden step until the air deepens
holds secateurs and non sequiturs

mandarins hum , sip nectar in
: all nature , a non-moving motion
. stability in , transience

o , mandarins fall sweet on earth
as childhood hiding in long grass
: cultivar-vowels drop t
o
silence

2 baghdad, 1980 / 2007

leaving the city, grey is dawning
a young eye looks up for the old
you that clings to dry seed-clouds

coming back (which is not return)
your memory scatters like pigeons
that will not feed from old hands

– 32nd parallel –

2015, prayer for charleston 1

in four directions let the body move
a hand   a dove

in four directions let the body move
a hand   a dove

in four directions let the body move
a hand   a dove

2 al-jalamah's orange trees

if a farmer weeps, he weeps for
three days—his heart uprooted
from between his lungs

roots and branches, leaves
and blossoms, pulled like scarves
from between his lungs

if the blossoms shake, a bee knocked
from a blossom—his tufted
bee body yellow with pollen,
the pollen that leapt to be
among his branching hairs

if the bee is knocked, he flees,
exiled—his hind leg heaving
a basket of pollen

if the pollen is heaved,
it is the last harvest—the harvest
of memory, the harvest
of song

– 31st parallel –

bird & fish world, gaza strip 1

shrapnel sears/
steel crows

and mr. al-draimli's cats have ears
soft as rose petals—and pink!

good for ages four & up
(esp. in cases of fear & fright)
telephone 2860098
or visit downtown al-wahdah street

they mew. they eat. they some days
look away from you with drawn
faces, as men in wrinkled shirts
without cigarettes or much hope

2 al-faraheen, gaza strip

after the disturbance, i gather
the small masses, fists forcing
out new purpose
and cupping it like a baby bird

the machines raze bullishly but
what of diesel, debris, and dust?
i gather

wheatdust, water: i'll show you
i'll show you hope in a handful
of dust

the way stars exploded offer up
new stars, my day's worth rises

stones we have thrown are stars
that lend no light
but mr. al-draimli's cats have
eyes—glittering black moons

nine times over, they will live
their lives in these cages, i think
mr. al-draimli's cats

my village queues and unshekels
herself, receives joyful; then

dry soil tautens to a foot drum
no night too aloof to witness

the processional of proud hands
each pair lifting ten suns

[redacted] persist as a "silent"

[redacted] persist [redacted]

ok

daniel

soon after you were born, doctors

scraped away each blue eye. early '80s;

the practice, *enucleation*—which the ear

registers as *atomic disaster,*

though it isn't.
& when for the first time

you removed before me the artifice,

sockets left naked, i might have turned

away, but i didn't. companions
for each other, each an imperfect

orb: acrylic, with vessels of red silk.
irides green & unmuted in their

lustre. we stood there by the bathroom sink,
passing the prostheses between us.

each bore the weight of a gold band. they fit
in our palms like two dice, a luckier hand.

postscript

– notes –

"poem for your pocket"
i will . . . come back

verses borrowed and stitched together from miklós radnóti's "letter to my wife" (trans. emery george), published in carolyn forché's *against forgetting: twentieth-century poetry of witness* (w. w. norton & company, 1993). source materials differ as to which pocket radnóti's notebook was found in—some citing the back pocket of his trousers, others citing his overcoat.

aries [the ram]
here . . . cross

verse borrowed from natasha tretheway's "fouled", published in *thrall* (houghton mifflin harcourt, 2012).

virgo (the virgin)
pas . . . terre

verses borrowed from derek walcott's "the light of the world". line breaks and repetition are my own.

"shirt"
frost-wrought silence

fragment borrowed and adapted from verses in john keats's "on the grasshopper and cricket": "when the frost / has wrought a silence".

"homecoming"
half . . . home

verse borrowed from w. s. merwin's "homecoming", published in *the moon before morning* (copper canyon press, 2014).

"letter"
from . . . i fell—

verse cut off and borrowed from randall jarrell's "the death of the ball turret gunner", published in *the complete poems* (farrar, straus and giroux, 1969).

"tending mint"

the impetus for this poem came from jen marlowe's 2011 documentary, *one family in gaza*, and from ellen bass's "moonlight", published in *like a beggar* (copper canyon press, 2014).

"susiya"	the impetus for this poem came from "even in the desert"—part two of b.h. yael's 2006 documentary, *palestine trilogy: documentations in history, land & hope.*
"she testifies" first half	for felicia solomon, delaine copenace, tina fontaine…
the damn… dead/	j.w. milam and roy bryant were arrested for and acquitted of the 1955 murder of emmett till, although, according to a 2005 article in *jackson free press*, "it was widely known that bryant and milam committed the crimes. … in october, [when they] could not be re-tried, [they] sold their confession to *look* magazine for $4,000, admitting to killing the boy" (http://www.jacksonfreepress.com/news/2005/nov/30/the-day-that-emmett-died). a 1985 *jackson daily news* article quotes roy bryant as saying, "he's been dead 30 years, and i can't see why it can't stay dead."
"– 43rd parallel –"	this poem is for sertaj shams and sandra edmunds. i could not have created this piece without your friendship or your generous provision of information during telephone interviews.
"– 42nd parallel –" first half	borrows language from dr. patrick jones's july 28th 2012 "garbling the gumweed" video (https://www.youtube.com/watch?v=uTPpWbqKZH4). i borrowed the diction "the worst dirt", "dry waste", and "no respect for soap & water".
our secret name	alludes to lucille clifton's "crabbing", which contains the lines: "meaning us / i imagine, / though our name / is our best secret" (*the book of light*, 1993).
second half	each line is a shortened version of something that lucille clifton's mother said to an audience of the then-depew-based macedonia baptist church when the poet was five: "she don't have to do nothing she don't want to do" (http://www.math.buffalo.edu/~sww/clifton/clifton-biobib.html).
"– 41st parallel –" burlap half	all lines from "they took" to "and i fell" were transcribed from a

2000 documentary called *threads of hope*, about the chilean *arpillera* movement. line breaks are my own.

canvas half

the italicized sentences from "*on the 3rd of january last*" to "*&c.*" are elided from a longer message published in *correspondence on slave trade with foreign powers: parties to conventions: under which vessels are to be tried by the tribunals of the nations to which they belong* (printed by william clowes and sons, stamford street, for her majesty's stationery office; london, 1842). line breaks are my own.

the fragments "had been a dressmaker" and "hands, small in life, / were very large and had / no fingernails" are found materials. i elided them from a longer passage published in inter-american commission on human rights's *third report on the situation of human rights in chile*, chapter 2: "right to life". line breaks are my own.

the spanish word *aparecida* means 'appeared one' (feminine).

"– 40th parallel –"

first half

text found, transcribed, and compressed from a video interview of 'natural builder' corwin mandel (http://www.livingbiginatinyhouse.com/natural-caravan-tiny-house). line breaks are my own.

second half

like the other italicized words in the third-last line of this poem, the word *sestina* can be created by rearranging the letters of islan nettles's name.

i am she : i am he

the fragments "i am she : i am he", "whose breasts still / bear the stress", and "the mermaid whose dark hair streams black / the merman in his unarmoured body" are adapted and/or stitched together from adrienne rich's poem, "diving into the wreck". line breaks are my own.

"– 38th parallel –"

first half

text fragments pieced together from the september 16th 2014 transcript of "grand jury: volume v" of the case *state of missouri v. darren wilson*. line breaks are my own.

second half

line breaks are my own.

"– 37th parallel –"

italicized passage — text found in and transcribed from lily cole's *vice* documentary, "lights in dark places" (https://video.vice.com/en_uk/video/light-in-dark-places/58ac23f28c0157477a35a73b). line breaks and formatting are my own.

i'm not sure if the speaker in the video was coming from kuşadası, but this city was, at the time of writing, one of the locations from which refugees were trying to make the short but treacherous voyage across the aegean.

"– 35th parallel –" — this poem is for parvaneh osmani and atsuko ueda.

without . . . kurds — kurdish proverb.

umi . . . tsukanai — japanese proverb: "it [a thing's true nature] belongs neither to the sea nor to the mountain". research taken from page 3 of daniel buchanan's *japanese proverbs and sayings* (university of oklahoma press, 1965).

"– 34th parallel –"

los angeles half — text from this half was adapted from *refinery29*'s interview of 'going with grace' founder alua arthur, "i graduated law school—& decided to become a 'death doula'" (https://www.refinery29.com/death-doula-meaning-career-advice).

clarksdale half — vera mae pigee was an african american, beauty-shop owner, and activist. at 407 ashton avenue, she kept her clients up to date about civil-rights struggles while she styled their hair and helped them with their voting-registration papers. due to the fact that men rarely entered this female domain, the salon became a covert and successful meeting place for civil-rights event organization. research taken from françoise n. hamlin's may 2011 article, "1961 in mississippi: beyond the freedom riders" (mississipi history now, http://mshistorynow.mdah.state.ms.us/articles/369/1961-in-mississippi-beyond-the-freedom-riders) and *mississippi today* (https://mississippitoday.org/2017/08/04/vera-mae-pigee-leader-in-the-fight-for-civil-rights-in-clarksdale).

"– 33rd parallel –" ehime half	inspired by japanese farmer and philosopher masanobu fukuoka's *the one-straw revolution.*
baghdad half	inspired by a *witness* documentary, *the poet of baghdad,* about nabeel yasin (https://www.youtube.com/watch?v=2roZyn1vS9o).
"– 32nd parallel –" *prayer for charleston*	although they don't fall along the 32nd parallel north, consider this half of the poem to also be *prayer for orlando* and *prayer for quebec city,* and on and on and on.
if… three days	the impetus for these verses came from an account by a man named faysal: "my father cried for three days straight when the orange trees were uprooted, because he considered our *bayara* (grove) and the trees like his children" (https://www.canaanusa.com/jalameh.php).
"– 31st parallel –" mr. al-draimli	shop owner featured in abigail hauslohner's october 7th 2009 *time* article, "raising cats in gaza: a pet store owner's lament" (http://content.time.com/time/world/article/0,8599,1927861,00.html).
diesel	diesel oven built by al-faraheen resident mohammed abu dagga, featured in eva bartlett's february 13th 2009 article, "no small enterprise: al faraheen's community bread oven" (https://ingaza.wordpress.com/2009/02/13/no-small-enterprise-al-faraheens-community-bread-oven).
i'll show you… dust	adapted from t.s. eliot's verses in *the waste land.*

– other than gratitude –

other than gratitude / so little survives the world's chronic revision—david bottoms

first publications } certain poems in *heft*—some with audio, some as previous iterations—were first published in: *academy of american poets's & league of canadian poets's 2017 poem in your pocket day booklet; arc poetry magazine; canadian notes & queries; canthius; contemporary verse 2; the fiddlehead; filling station; in/words magazine; kenyon review online; pelorus press; peter f. yacht club; prism international; the puritan; split rock review; this magazine; the unpublished city (volume one); and valley voices: a literary review.* thank you to the editors and teams of all of these journals for expending extra time and energy to preserve finicky formatting.

reprints & broadsheets } "site" and "sites" were reprinted in *another dysfunctional cancer poem anthology.* "– 31st parallel –" was reprinted in the *best canadian poetry in english, 2018.* the second half of "– 32nd parallel –" was reprinted in league of canadian poets's *heartwood* anthology. "jelera" (previously titled "the fishermen") and "trip to yarl's wood" were reprinted in *the manifesto project,* along with my poetry manifesto, "a private architecture of resistance". "poem for your pocket" and "– 32nd parallel –" were republished through league of canadian poets's *poetry pause* initiative. thank you to the editors, guest editors, publishers, and proofreaders of all of these anthologies. thank you, also, to briar craig for printing "cat and door" as a limited-edition artisan broadsheet.

awards, contests, & prizes } *arc poetry magazine* awarded "site" the title of 2016 poem of the year. (don't worry, i wasn't working there yet!) *contemporary verse 2* and guest judge sara peters awarded "two burials" first place in the 2015 young buck poetry prize. *contemporary verse 2* awarded "– 35th parallel –" first place in its 2010 thirty-fifth anniversary contest. league of canadian poets and guest judge sharon thesen selected "cat and door" as the winner of the inaugural national broadsheet contest. *arc poetry magazine* nominated the poems "bhater mondo", "– 32nd parallel –", and "– 31st parallel –" for the 2017 national magazine awards. *contemporary verse 2* nominated "water for canaries" for the 2017 national magazine awards. judges wayde compton, brigitte trudel, and sina queyras selected me as a poetry finalist for the

2017 national magazine awards for the poems "bhater mondo", "– 32nd parallel –", and "– 31st parallel –". thank you.

fellowships & grants } i am grateful for the financial support of the following organizations, and grateful to the juries and editors who advocated for this manuscript while it was a work in progress: ontario arts council in conjunction with the chalmers family fund (chalmers arts fellowship, 2015); canada council for the arts (grants for professional writers program, 2013); ontario arts council in conjunction with brick books, guernica, and wolsak & wynn (recommender grants for writers, 2017); ontario arts council in conjunction with brick books (writers' reserve program, 2014); and barbara deming memorial fund (money for women program, 2014).

radio & skype convs } thank you to michael enright of cbc radio's *the sunday edition* for interviewing me about *heft* and my poetics in general, and for letting me share "poem for your pocket" and "cat and door" on air in 2017. thank you to laurie kruk for facilitating my reading of and skype dialogue around the poem "site" with students of nipissing university's 'family in literature' course in 2016. thank you to pearl pirie for inviting me to read the poem "jelera" (previously titled "the fishermen") and to discuss my poetry on ckcu fm's *literary landscape* in 2016.

text convs } thank you to the following people for dialoguing with me about the poems in *heft*, and about my wider practice, and thank you to the following spaces for publishing the conversations: forrest gander (*the adroit journal*); natalie hanna (*arc poetry magazine* e-newsletter); anne michaels (*contemporary verse 2*); natalya anderson (the poetry extension); mirae lee (project 40 collective blog); rob mclennan (rob mclennan's blog); toronto international festival of authors; and e martin nolan (*the town crier*). thank you, also, to jennifer hosein for mentioning "bhater mondo" in her own project 40 collective 'creator-to-creator' interview, with a beautiful illustration to reflect the spirit of the poem.

performance } audio excerpts from the poem "– 43rd parallel –" were featured in *dusk society*, a 2017 dusk dances performance by dancer/choreographer rhodnie désir and music producer engone endong.

festivals & readings } i thank shazia hafiz ramji, selina boan, and jessica johns for giving me the opportunity to share some of this work at the *prism international* launch in 2018. i thank alvin wong for inviting me to share some of these poems at crossroads literary festival at york university in 2018. i thank sanchari sur for giving me the opportunity to share some of this work at balderdash reading series in 2017. i thank claire farley and cira nickel for giving me the opportunity to share "she testifies", "poem for your pocket", "susiya", "bhater mondo", and "– 32nd parallel –" at the *canthius* launch of issue 2 in toronto in 2017. i thank *pelorus press*, in conjunction with the creators collective, for giving me the opportunity to share "moving day" and a draft of "– 40th parallel –" in brooklyn in 2017. i thank speakeasy and simone dalton for giving me the opportunity to read "– 43rd parallel –" at the steady in 2017. i thank maggie helwig for giving me the opportunity to share some of this work at bread and honey in 2016. i thank charles c. smith and sheniz janmohamed for facilitating the university of toronto scarborough buddhist-sufi poetry reading, during which i shared some of these poems in 2016. i thank anne michaels for giving me the opportunity to share some of this work at the 2016 east end poetry festival. i thank co-editors lise rochefort and sanita fejzić of *in/words magazine* for giving me the opportunity to share some of this work at the 2016 ottawa international writers festival. i thank jacob mcarthur mooney for featuring me at pivot readings in 2016 in toronto, where i shared some of this work. i thank susie berg and rod weatherbie for featuring me through plasticine poetry series, where i shared some of this work in 2016. i thank monty reid and the organizers of versefest 2016 for giving me the opportunity to share some of these poems in ottawa. i thank roger nash for inviting me to read some of these poems at sudbury writers monthly open mic at greater sudbury public library in 2015.

– i am chronically grateful –

to my ancestors, for arriving me.

to my maternal grandmother, who took the pen name nurun nahar.

to my family, for no one is self-sufficient. thank you to my mother, shirin islam, for your sweetness & unfathomable labour "all these year / all these years". thank you to my father, mohammad rafiqul islam, for the expansiveness of your thought, & for our listening game. thank you to my sister, laboni islam, for the acts of care that i see & do not see.

to my human friends, for the sharing of kitchen-table meals, kindness, & poetry.

to poncho the cat, for being the most wondrous creature in the universe, the friendliest friend, & my muse in north bay. i scattered your whiskers—which clung to carpet & rocking chair—in the woods behind millwood junior school. may you perch on the highest branch & sniff the fresh air.

to my m&s family: dionne brand, for feeling the heft of it & for pushing me to write more; kelly joseph, for the immense grace of your person & for holding open a line of communication built on trust & listening; rachel cooper, for the attention with which you designed *heft*'s interiors, & for building a cover that i love; sean tai, for typesetting these finicky poems; peter norman, for copy editing/proofreading with such care; valentina capuani, for your conscientiousness; kimberlee hesas, for being a mastermind; erin kelly, for your thoughtful & creative voicing; joe lee, for your many hats; bridgette kam, for your attentiveness; anita chong, for truly seeing me in rooms; jared bland, for your keen input at crucial times, which allowed me to reconsider & set right the title of this book. book production is an art in itself, & i thank everyone else at m&s who has had a hand in producing & illuminating *heft*.

to sylvia legris, for your continued support, & for being the first to recognize my work & open a door.

to anne michaels, for your generous support.

to amanda ghazale aziz, for our conversation that afternoon at l'espresso bar mercurio.

to conspiracy of 3, where i first learned the meaning of community.

to forces seen & unseen.

to all those who have had long flights into their bodies, & who show their resourcefulness & resilience.

to anyone who feels witnessed within "vulva" or "v". i risked this terrain for you.

to daniel zingaro, in whose copy of *heft* i will cover over, with a strip of braille, the following insight:

it is only with the heart that one can see rightly—antoine de saint-exupéry

to my body for yielding these poems, including the ten 'inversas' that form a latitude line of my body.

& to you, dear reader-listener, for leaning in with the meridian of your body—

MICHELLE GU 2018

DOYALI ISLAM's poems have been published in *Kenyon Review Online*, *The Fiddlehead*, and *The Best Canadian Poetry in English*, and have won several national contests and prizes. Doyali serves as the poetry editor of *Arc Poetry Magazine*. In 2017, she was a guest on CBC Radio's *The Sunday Edition* and was a poetry finalist for the National Magazine Awards. She lives in Toronto, Ontario. *heft* is her second collection of poetry.